What Tomorrow May Hold

What Tomorrow May Hold

Asperger's From A Teen's View

Nicolas Saliani

While every precaution has been taken in the preparation of this book, the publisher assumes no responsibility for errors or omissions, or for damages resulting from the use of the information contained herein.

™©*Mickey Mouse* and ™ *PAC-MAN belong to their respective owners.*

WHAT TOMORROW MAY HOLD

First Edition. May 24, 2016

Copyright © 2016 Nicolas Saliani

Written by Nicolas Saliani

All rights reserved.
ISBN: 0692726012
ISBN-13: 978069276013

Dedicated

To my friend, Adhy
& everyone facing
challenges in their lives.

Contents

1 A Short Introduction 1

2 Asperger's and Me 3

3 The Autism Spectrum 9

4 Every Day's a Staircase 13

5 A Little More About Myself 18

6 Daycare 30

7 Elementary School 40

8 Middle School 71

9 The Stairs Collapse 77

10 Tomorrow 93

Acknowledgements

I would like to thank all the people who helped and supported me while I wrote this book. Special thanks to Jennifer Kaut and Mellissa Bower.

Cites: Chances of being born with autism
www.cdc.gov

Foreword

By the end of the first page, you will know that this book is unlike any other you have read. Nicolas takes your hand and invites you to come along as he gives you a glimpse into the world of Autism. He draws you in by including you in every conversation. Together you laugh out loud at people's inability to use correct grammar rules, lose patience with a teacher who clearly does not know the definition of a library, find solace as coping skills are found, and discover that life is truly full of limitless possibilities. You will want to high five him for his hysterical responses to people, hope that he never sees your terrible grammar habits, and walk away with a perspective of Autism that you will never forget. By the last page of this book, you will conclude that you have just met the world's next gifted genius who will make a lasting impact on whatever he puts his mind to.

Jennifer
Jennifer Kaut M.Ed., BCBA
Board Certified Behavior Analyst
State Autism & Developmental Disorders Specialist
Department of Assistive and Rehabilitation Services | DRS

1 A Short Introduction

Hey there. I don't believe we've met. My name is Nicolas Saliani. I'm 13 years old, and I have what's called Asperger's syndrome. You may or may not know what this is, but I'll talk about it very soon. Now, I'm just a teenager. What's so important about me? How am I so special? How come I can write a memoir about growing up with Asperger's? It's not common for someone with Asperger's to be able to talk about their feelings. I have a gift, and I can use it to bring a better understanding to not only Asperger's, but to autism itself.

First, do you know about Asperger's syndrome? If you do know about Asperger's but don't have it, then this book is about a teen that lives with it every day. If you have it, then maybe you can relate to some of the things I talk about. If you do not even have an inkling about it, then sit tight. It's been a long journey so far.

(DISCLAIMER: Some names of people in this book have been changed to protect their identities.)

(DISCLAIMER #2: Not everything in this book is chronological. Some things I talk about may apply to a later time in my life, but be referenced before another time. For example, I talk about what I was like as a child in school before I talk about when I moved into school. So just an FYI.)

2 Asperger's and Me

Disclaimer: If there are parents reading this book that are struggling to raise children with Asperger's, listen. READ THE SECTION BELOW. PLEASE. I am a child. What I talk about here is all about Asperger's and autism. I also talk about what having Asperger's is like being A KID. The most valuable thing to know when helping to raise a child with Asperger's is what's going on inside their head. If you know that, you can help them tremendously. I can give you that in this book. Absorb the knowledge that you think is valuable, take my advice that you think may help, and read on.

What is Asperger's? A fantabulous question. Asperger's is a mild form of autism where people who have it might be extremely smart, but have severe trouble being socially appropriate. For example, a young kid with Asperger's might have a hard time making friends because he gets angry when his peers won't share their toys with him. But, he could have skipped a grade because he knew more than he could be taught in kindergarten. To sum it up, Asperger's can be a blessing and a curse. Most of the blessing comes in knowledge and academics. They may have an increased IQ; maybe know a little about a lot of things, and probably WAY ahead in math and language arts. But, some of the curse kicks in when they interact with others. They may have problems managing their anger, maybe they don't filter their thoughts, they probably don't make eye contact, and maybe get anxious easily. You can know when an aspie (term for someone with Asperger's) might be getting anxious when they start performing repetitive or unorthodox rituals or behaviors.

For example, they might wring their hands, swing their arms, or pace around a room. Whenever I'm listening to someone talk at home, I'll pace around the room that we're in. I still listen, but that's just what I do.

Aspies do this to calm their anxiety. I sometimes snap my fingers when I get anxious. The only difference is I learned to snap super-diddly fast with four fingers, so I use my ring finger and middle finger on both hands in sequence to make a very fast snapping sound. And sometimes I might not even be anxious. I just like to practice doing that.

There is a big difference with Asperger's compared to most other forms of autism. Asperger's is incurable, just like all other forms of autism, but the "curse", or bad part of Asperger's can actually be worked around. It's not quick and easy; trust me on this, but it can yield great rewards like... *dun DUN* Being able to communicate like everyone else! Think I'm joking? That's because not everyone reading this is too acquainted with Asperger's. Being able to interact socially is a HUGE deal for people with Asperger's, and is more valuable to us than it is for most people.

I have had to work a lot on myself to get to where I am today. Of course with much help from others. Not only am I smart, but my social skills have improved MUCH beyond where they were when I was younger. Sometimes when my mom and I are out somewhere, people will tell my mom that they would have never even known I had Asperger's if she didn't tell them. Don't get me wrong, though. I'm not perfect. Far from it, actually. I still have things about me I need to work on. Not all of the curse is gone; I'm still the aspie I've always been. This is okay though, because it makes me who I am. What am I? I'm smart, talented, and most of all, sarcastic.

Those first two may sound like narcissistic things to say, and I agree. It's really hard for me to compliment myself like that because I do it so rarely, and that's because I'm extraordinarily hard on myself. (More on that later.) That and it seems like everyone says they're smart because there apparently aren't any dumb people anymore. That last sentence was a sample of my type of sarcasm. It can be funny when used in the right situation, but I have a habit of using inappropriate sarcasm that isn't only used at the wrong time, but it's the type that I should keep to myself.

Kids who haven't worked on their Asperger's almost NEVER filter thoughts like that. If they think about something, they will probably say it. This isn't because they're rude, but because they don't have an understanding about what's appropriate to say to others and what's not. To them, it's all the same. There are a few other things aspies have trouble with: Reading people's faces, recognizing emotions or feelings (being sympathetic or empathetic), eye contact, and controlling their thoughts, actions, and feelings. These four things are things most people can do fine, which is why they're considered socially normal or adept. Aspies have issues with all four of these things, which is why they can be considered socially abnormal or inept.

Let me list several important things about Aspies.

1. They mostly have trouble interacting socially. A child with Asperger's may be socially active, but they're a little awkward. This is not a bad thing, but it can be worked on.
2. They have trouble with eye contact. I used to have a hard time looking people in the eyes. I don't remember much of that time, but it probably made me feel uncomfortable or stressed. This isn't a big problem.
3. They have difficulty empathizing. Aspies are not senseless, they just have trouble empathizing. If, say, their friend is upset and they're talking to him, the aspie might not REALLY know why their friend is upset. This can be an issue when they're playing with friends, and the aspie won't know

when to stop doing something that people don't like. Luckily, aspies learn how to empathize as they age.

4. They have very specific interests. An aspie might be very interested about certain things, like art or planes. They might go on and on about one topic that they know about. This isn't limited to just knowledge, as they may like to do things like play video games or draw. When I say aspies are smart, I'm not saying that they all do fantastic in school. I'm saying that they know a lot about different things.

5. They stick to routines. A schedule is a good example.

3 The Autism Spectrum

Asperger's is a form of autism. What is autism? Well, it's hard to explain, so allow me to start like this. Autism or ASD (Autism Spectrum Disorder) is a type of neurological disorder that usually originates from heredity. The chances of being born with autism are not very low; in fact, it's been growing for years: The (CDC) states that in the year 2014, 1/68 children will be identified on the Autism Spectrum. That statistically means if you were to line up 68 newborn babies, at least one of them will have a form of autism. The easiest way to understanding autism would be to have some sort of visual stimuli.

Autism itself "looks" like a spectrum, which is why autism is scientifically referred to as ASD, or Autism Spectrum Disorder. The reason it can be referred to that way is because autism has many different "symptoms", as mentioned earlier. Though, autism isn't just Asperger's: it varies in severity, which is what I'm going to talk about here.

First, imagine the autism spectrum as sort of a rainbow. The left side of the rainbow is the low-functioning side. People on this side of the spectrum function at a low scale. I have a cousin that my family and I visit occasionally. He is on the low functioning side of the rainbow. He cannot speak, he communicates nonverbally, he cannot go to the bathroom without assistance, etc. What he mostly does all day is rock back and forth on the couch and makes noises. No one knows what goes on inside his head, but it isn't enough to the point where he can live on his own and care for himself on his own. Some "disorders" on the low-functioning side of the rainbow are "milder" on the autism. They won't really be able to speak, but they can process their thoughts to a larger degree. Some people can't function very well, but they can use a keyboard to communicate with others. Unfortunately, some people with Autism lack motor skills and the basic skills needed to understand most ethics and reasoning capabilities to move past the point where they are.

With some people on the left side, they can still communicate through things other than speaking. They're still them on the inside, they are conscious of what they are doing and what they are thinking. And just because some of them are able to communicate like the rest of us, it doesn't mean that their intelligence stops there. So some people on the left side of the rainbow can still function, but not with all of the "left-siders".

The right side of the rainbow involves mild forms of autism, like Asperger's syndrome. Asperger's is actually so out there as a form of autism that some scientists debate Asperger's shouldn't even be considered autism; it should be considered a league of its own and not on the spectrum at all.

Well, that's Asperger's for ya. But in reality that description barely even scratches the surface of what Asperger's really is. If you want to know the most about Asperger's, you want to read this book. So If you don't mind, I'm gonna tell you my life story. This is only what I can remember at best, and what has happened in my life so far. Near the end, it will become more like a diary, as the more I write the book, the closer it will get to the present. If there are any parents reading this book right now that are struggling with a child with Asperger's, you're going to find out what it's like inside of the head of one. That goes out to basically everyone reading this.

What I'm gonna state first is that it was NOT easy growing up. I'm only 13 now, so knowing that you can jam-pack so much into 13 years frightens me. I'm gonna start off by telling you the first things I can remember growing up, so stick around for the story, because you might just learn something.

4 Every Day's a Staircase

I was born on February 19, 2002. I was apparently supposed to be born on a leap year, so if I was, I would only be about 4 right now. As a baby, I always wanted to see everything. I would not stop turning my head around, because I just wanted to see everything around me. As my mom would put it, someone was gonna fart, and I was gonna miss it. I moved my head so much that I eventually got a rash on the back of my neck. My mom took me to the doctor, and the doctor only said that I was just very curious. At around 11 months old, I was even more curious.

Whenever my dad sat down to use the computer, I would monkey-crawl over to him, get in front of him, and start pushing all the keys on the keyboard. As in, take over. My dad was pretty much powerless to keep doing what he was doing after that. My parents had to get me my own little special, colorful keyboard that went over the regular keyboard. It had a bunch of different shapes on each key, so if I pushed the key that had a circle, it would actually push the spacebar underneath. There was also a disc that came with it that acted as a program for the keyboard. For example, if I pushed the key with a square, a little sailboat would go by on the screen. If I pushed the triangle, the kite would change colors, etc. I sat in there for hours playing on that little keyboard. My mom had read an article around that time that talked about the common functionalities of a child around my age. It stated things like 'at about 6 months old, your child should be growing their first teeth, and begin to teeth on things.' There was one page she read that said 'At around 11 months old, your child should have a maximum attention span of around 10-20 minutes.' After she read that, she realized that I had been in my dad's office for about 3 hours.

Remember, this was before I could even walk. So, we quickly found out that I could remain occupied for much longer than the average three-year-old, and I wasn't even two yet. Children with Asperger's tend to have a very large attention span for almost anything they enjoy.

At around six months old, I learned to communicate in a somewhat special way. To communicate, I would use hand motions to say what I wanted. One of them was where I would shake my hands, and that meant "done". If my mom was swinging me on the swing, I would be doing fine, and then all of the sudden I'd shake my hands, and I'd be done. Next thing. Done. Next thing. It was kind of sudden at times. My parents taught me to do this whenever I'd try to say I was done with something. So whenever I would grunt and try to get out of the swing, my dad would say, "Are you 'done', Nic? Are you 'done'?" and make the hand motions at the same time she said done, putting emphasis on the word "done" as well. I caught on quickly and started using the gesture to say "I'm done" without using actual words. For a six-month-old, this is VERY advanced. My parents also taught me basic words when I was six months old, using the same technique. Whenever I'd grunt and gesture for, say, an apple, my dad would pick up the apple, point to it, and say, "Do you want the 'apple', Nic? The 'apple'?" With this method I learned some basic words pretty quickly. In fact, my dad still has a list of all the words I knew and used when I was six months old.

When I spoke my first word, my mom and dad were sitting in their bedroom with me, waiting for me to say something. Mom was saying, "Say 'mama', Nic. Say 'mama'!" and Dad was saying, "Say 'dada', Nic. Say 'dada'!" I sat there for a while, and eventually, I said "Dada." Dad immediately threw his hands up in the air in a fist-pumping motion. Mom says she's always been jealous that I said "Dada" first.

Like I said earlier, I had a very long attention span back then, like most kids with Asperger's have. Whenever my friends came to play, they would be doing this thing, and then that thing over there, basically they got bored quickly. "I wanna do that now," they said. "Now that." Meanwhile I just played with Matchbox cars for hours on end. I would line up Matchbox cars in certain places. Usually on the windowsill, because that was where I usually played with my cars and my trains. I would line up the cars in a certain pattern, for example, a rainbow. And they could not be just any old cars, no. it would have to be very certain ones, so I would go digging in the huge "Bin O' Cars", and find the exact cars I wanted. And then I would line them up juuuust right. Sometimes I would line them up in the most random places, even right smack-dab in the middle of the living room. And DO NOT even TOUCH them or move them in any way, shape or form. Sometimes my parents would just barely even nudge one with their toe, and they'd be frantic over putting it back just the way it was before. Otherwise, I'd have a meltdown. A perfectionist back then, a perfectionist for life.

5 A Little More About Myself

So, yes, kids with Asperger's can have repetitive habits, or "rituals". Want to know some of mine? I would line up the dog food for some of the dogs I had when I was younger. I would pick out their food and line them up across the kitchen floor in a pattern with all of the different kibble designs. I even ate some dog food once out of curiosity. My parents called poison control, but they said it was no big deal. (I once even called 911 by myself on accident. I was no more than one, and the police even showed up.)

Want another? I liked to count garage doors. My parents would drive me down streets and I would examine the garage doors people had. I would have little names and words for certain ones, too. If someone had one garage door, I had a name for that. If someone had one garage door with windows on it, that would be another thing. If someone had two different garage doors, but one was currently open, I had a name for THAT, too. Think of any combination of garage door; I probably had a name for it. I would do this for minutes on end, ranging from thirty minutes to an hour. I enjoyed doing it, too. I would be excited if a combination I liked showed up, or if we went by a house I liked, or if I saw a new combination I had never seen before. I did this a lot, too. Whenever my friends' parents called my dad, and we were occupied counting garage doors, they wouldn't even be confused. "Hey, can the boys hang out today?" "Yeah, I'm just driving Nic around; he's counting garage doors." "So, maybe in, like, an hour?" "Yeah, sounds good." So I had repetitive habits when I was younger. Unorthodox or not, I had them, and it especially doesn't matter if a child with

Asperger's has a really weird habit. Any child with Asperger's probably has at least one odd habit.

Here's another thing about aspies: they can NOT read emotions. I've had training with reading emotions, and I'm really good at it now; maybe even better than most people. But when I was little, I couldn't read emotions at all. This includes eyes, tone, body language, and even facial expressions. One day, when I was very young, I was at a friend's birthday party, waiting in line to play a game. For whatever reason, I decided to shove the boy in front of me. Mom was talking with some other women when she saw this happen. She waited for me to look at her, and then she made a face at me that said "Stop it." When I looked at her face, it deeply confused me. This was so confusing to me that I stepped out of line, walked over to Mom, and asked, "What's wrong with your face, Mommy?" Mom said, "I was making that face to tell you to stop pushing that boy." I said, "Oh. Okay," and then left to get back in line. This moment shows how far I've come in terms of reading emotions.

I liked trains. A lot. Really, you have no clue. I REALLY liked trains. It stayed that way for many years, and I'm still fond of trains today. I had DVDs of live-action trains and I would just watch them all the time. I had little toy trains that I would play with for hours. I even had some of those toy trains lying right next to me in my bed so I could play with them before I fell asleep. Yes, I was way into trains. Especially the toys. The certain toy trains I liked were a kind that my parents and I bought from a local toy store. They weren't very cheap, either. They cost about twenty dollars apiece. If I had my sights on a train that I wanted, I'd whine until my parents bought it. Yeah, I know, I was spoiled. I ended up practically sucking the money out of my parents' pockets. I don't think my parents minded too much, though, because we laugh about it today.

The reason I would get angry if my parents didn't buy something for me isn't because I was spoiled, but because I was still struggling with Asperger's. That may sound like an excuse now, but let me try to explain it the best I can. I didn't know what was socially acceptable, so I'd throw fits about a lot of things. I would throw fits if I didn't win something, I'd throw fits if something didn't go my way, and I'd throw fits if my parents didn't buy those trains. I was still very young, so my social skills weren't as developed as some kids' were yet. So I just wanted to make that clear. I wasn't a spoiled little brat. I was struggling with Asperger's.

Speaking of which, I don't like to lose. Most people don't. But when I was younger, I would have a meltdown over losing. I always wanted to win everything. Today, I can control my emotions over losing a lot better than I could, but depending on how I lost, I may juggle it in my mind for a while. If I lost a game in a way that I felt was cheap, I might perseverate, or think about over and over, about that moment. I do this mainly to think in depth about what exactly happened so I can comprehend everything. After I comprehend it, I try to get the thought out of my mind, as when I start perseverating, it's hard for me to stop. To do this, I try to get my mind on something else. One thing I tell myself sometimes is this: "Losing doesn't make you any less of a man; it makes you more of a person." Maybe that's silly. I don't know. But it may help someone out there.

When I was around two years old, I made my first two friends. My mom and I were playing in the front yard, and our neighbor to our right drove into their driveway. My mom knew they had little kids, so she grabbed my hand and we walked over and stood behind a large hedge that separated our yard from theirs. They usually entered their house through the garage, but this time, they were using the front door. This was Mom's chance. She popped out from behind the hedge with me and introduced us to our neighbors. The mom had two small boys, and we arranged a "playdate". Soon after, I ended up becoming good friends with those boys. When they would come over to my house, we would all run around the couch while my dad played a certain tune on the guitar. We always did that for a long time. I became especially good friends with the younger of the two boys, and he even ended up being in my first grade class. Unfortunately, when I was only in second grade, they had to move all the way to California. My family and I still keep in touch with them.

I was very literal back then, meaning I took everything in a literal sense. Metaphors and expressions were the bane of my understanding. One day my mom came home from work, and she said, "My feet are killing me!" I heard her say that, and I said, "...Don't die!" I was very worried that Mom was really going to die, and she had to explain to me what she meant. So, I know the real meaning of literal, and it gets on my nerves whenever someone uses the word "literally" incorrectly.

That's another thing: I really like to correct people. I believe smart people LOVE to correct others. Whenever someone makes a mistake in pronunciation, grammar, spelling, or fact, I must correct them, and I can rarely EVER keep myself from correcting them. ESPECIALLY spelling. Whenever someone spells ANYTHING wrong, I must correct them. Sometimes my mom even shows me pictures of absurd misspellings, and we have a laugh over it. This trait only applies to me now, because I just don't remember correcting many people when I was younger.

I learned a lot from the people around me, including attitude. I would see my mom and how she would talk to me when I got in trouble, and I'd reflect that back. So I'd say, "No, mama! Bad!" Or, "Mama, listen to me." Then after I finished and she said something I didn't agree with, I'd say "You're not listening to me! Listen!"

I was also very stubborn back then. I'd always say "I can do it," whenever I tried to do something I really couldn't do. Well, most of the time I couldn't do it. So if I was doing something too hard, my mom would ask if she could do it for me, and I'd say, "No, mama! No! I can do it!" So she'd let me fail and she would try. There was, however, one thing I learned to do pretty quickly.

I learned to read when I was around three years old. My family discovered this when my mom was riding me around in a shopping cart inside of the local grocery store, and she heard me talking. She thought that I was just repeating words that I knew. Eventually, she turned around to find that I was reading what I saw around me. I'd be reading things like "Cookies", "Beans", "Crackers", even "Express Checkout", by myself.

Whenever it was bedtime, my mom and dad would read me a book. She always had to point to the word she was on. If I didn't see what word she was on, I'd stop her and ask where the word was. "'Important'. Where is 'important'? Where is it?" And she would point to where the word "important" was. Then, I would hold the book inches from my face and study the word like I was trying to burn 'important' into my memory. And for a decent amount of time, too. So we'd be lying there while I'm staring at the book for 5 seconds, and then I'd say, "...'Important'. ...Okay." And I would give the book back.

So my parents found out that I could read on my own. I was at a friend's house playing a board game one day, and their parents volunteered to help me read the cards. I said "I can do it," and I read the card by myself. It said something like "Move two spaces forward."

There was also a day where I was at church and I read a bible verse to my peers by myself. So soon enough everyone was asking my mom "Did you know he could read?" and she'd always reply "Yes."

Now, not everything about me was perfect, of course. If I haven't made that clear in the last several paragraphs, let me share with you how I was when I was a little one.

I had sensory issues. Meaning, if my clothes didn't feel right or comfortable enough, it drove me up the freakin' wall. If I was getting dressed, and one little thing wasn't just right, I would have to start over. I would take off ALL of my clothes and start from the blank canvas that was my naked body. Yes. I would usually do this when I had to put my socks and shoes on. One sensory issue I had and still have with socks is that there can't be a seam across the toe. I hate that. It makes the sock very uncomfortable. So I'd almost be out the door, and all I'd have left were my socks, and if I put them on and decide they "didn't feel right", I would take off everything. Just the socks would have sufficed, but NOOO. New socks, new shirt, new pants, everything. It still bugs me if I wear jeans or have small shirts. The zippers and buttons on the jeans make them feel tight and uncomfortable all around. The small shirts are self-explanatory, though my version of "small" is "just right" for most others. I like the shirt to cover my waist and not end just below the seam of the pants. Otherwise, I think it's too short to go out with and I put on a new shirt.

Here's something that's very important about me. I'm very sympathetic. I apply my feelings towards others. This includes inanimate objects or fictional situations. When I was little, I had these little disposable cups that I used to wash my mouth out after I brushed my teeth. Only I didn't throw them out because I thought they'd feel bad. I applied my feelings toward an inanimate object. Even though they can't feel, I imagined they could. Eventually a pile of cups started to stack up by the windowsill. I refused to throw them away. At some point I did finally throw them away, but it was a slow process. Mom slowly started throwing them out day by day after I said it was okay. Another example is that I loved stuffed animals. I had SO many stuffed animals, and I loved each and every one of them. I always kept them on my bed, and if any fell off, I'd bring them back up. I took the ones I loved the most on road trips, and I felt bad for the ones I didn't take. I wanted them to feel loved. If they felt bad, I felt bad. Or rather, I felt bad if I thought THEY would feel bad. I still have lots of stuffed animals now, but I keep them in my closet because they take up the bed. So how does this apply to me today?

  I still feel sympathy for inanimate objects, like trash on the side of the road or stuffed animals. Sometimes, even food. I feel bad for food that I don't eat. But here's what I feel most sympathy for: imaginary situations. If I see a bad situation in a game, movie, or in my own head, I transfer myself into that scenario and I try to feel what could be felt. This isn't good, because I don't need to do it, I can't HELP doing it, and because it makes me extremely anxious. Sometimes I think, "What would I feel if I were trapped in a dark space?" I then think of what it would be like to be trapped in a dark space, and it makes me anxious because I can imagine what it would be like. This usually happens against my will. I don't want to do it, but I can't help thinking about it. It could be a normal day without anything to fear, and suddenly, I'd think about bad thoughts and begin to freak out and get anxious. To counter this I usually try to stay away from anything that might freak me out or trigger me in any way. To stop it, I try to get my mind on something else or get out of the house. Thankfully, this rarely happens at school. If it does, it usually ends after a couple classes. Sorry, I've foreshadowed a little bit. No matter. I'll catch up now.

6 Daycare

When I was about three months old, I began going to a daycare center. As you may expect, I didn't do too much, because I was three months old. I would just play and sleep in this little room with teachers and other small children. I hated staying in the crib. The daycare person would put me in the swing, hold me or let me have "tummy time" on the floor. My crib at the daycare ended up being filled with toys since I needed more stimulation than lying in a bed.

As I grew older, I would move into different rooms with different teachers and kids. Whenever I transitioned between these rooms, it was stressful for everyone. I hated change. Most aspies probably do. I'm still not too fond of change today. For example, we're getting a new carpet in the living room, and I want it to look similar to the one that's in there now, because it's been there for years and I've grown up with it. I also have trouble re-arranging my room (when the time ever comes) because I have to get used to it being different all over again. Anyway, back to the story. I would get angry whenever I would have to change rooms because I had to get used to a new teacher, new kids, a new room, and it just felt overwhelming to me. So, I would just take out my anger on the new things. I would say to the teacher, "Go away," or, "I hate you," even when I really didn't, and I would have a hard time making new friends. I would get angry at the room if something was different about it. One room I moved into had the numbers 1-20 across the top of the wall, and I was angry that it didn't go any higher. My previous room had the same sort of thing, but the numbers went higher and I could count higher than twenty.

After a couple of transitions, I met a teacher that I really did like when I was 4 years old. I liked him, I liked his room, and I liked spending time with him. I wasn't the easy-going hyper little tyke like everyone else. I was more quiet and intellectual. Whenever the kids would go outside to play, I would stay inside with the teacher and draw or play with toys while I listened to classical music.

That teacher was one of the first teachers to really understand me, and THE first teacher to tell my parents that there was something different about me. He told them that I wasn't like the other kids and that I was very smart. Taking this into mind, my parents started investigating more into my behavior. Being very smart but having a fit whenever anything bad happened was an odd mixture of traits that was far from run-of-the-mill. Soon my parents found a psychologist that didn't only help me immensely, but helped to give my parents a better understanding of my challenges and traits. His name was Dr. Gay.

Dr. Gay was a very nice man. He was soft-spoken and never yelled or raised his voice. He eased whatever mood that was in the room. He was also very smart and communicated with my parents well. In one of the first appointments we had with Dr. Gay, my parents told him there was something odd about me, and they didn't know what to do. Around this time I grew attached to drawing various things. Whenever I was drawing and, say, a teacher told everyone, "Alright, time's up! Drawing time is over," and I wasn't done yet, I'd throw a fit. So Dr. Gay conducted a little experiment.

He sat at a desk across from me, and he gave me a sheet of paper. He then said I could start drawing the letters of the alphabet that I knew. I started drawing the letters of the alphabet and got very into it. Then Dr. Gay suddenly flipped the sheet over and said, "Okay, now start drawing your numbers." I was angry. I told him that I wasn't done with my letters over and over, and then started throwing a fit. He then flipped the sheet over again, and said, "Okay, you can finish drawing your letters." So I started drawing my letters again. Dr. Gay turned towards my parents and said, "He needs more time to transition, or something to let him know what's about to happen. Give him a heads up when something's going to change. If he's drawing, tell him he has five more minutes, and then it's time to stop and do something else." My parents were pretty surprised. This new information was a huge help and really eased tension in sudden change. It even works today, and I'm grateful for that. My parents will tell me, "Ten minutes and then you have to wash your face and brush your teeth," or "Five minutes and it's time to come in the room and watch TV."

(Side note: I watch TV in my parents' room before I go to bed.)

For the next visit my parents told Dr. Gay about a new issue. Whenever I might be drawing, and it wasn't coming out the way I wanted it to, I would tear up the sheet of paper and begin drawing on myself. Sometimes if a teacher was walking by and was about to look at my drawing, I would tear it up before they could look at it. The teachers all said that my drawings looked perfect, but I still tore up my drawings and proceeded to draw on myself. Dr. Gay said that I was a perfectionist, and if I couldn't get something just right, or just the way I wanted it, I would get angry at myself, and consider myself a failure. He said that when the teachers told me that my drawings were perfect, I took word of it. So when I drew something I didn't like, I'd think, 'If I'm perfect, why can't I draw properly?' and tear it up. Dr. Gay said to tell me not that my drawings were perfect, but to instead say, 'I like how hard you tried.' After my parents and teachers started telling me that, I stopped drawing on myself and stopped tearing up papers as often. Dr. Gay also told my parents to NEVER tell me 'practice makes perfect', because I'd get angry when I couldn't get it right.

Dr. Gay also helped my parents out with a different issue. I hated to lose. If I lost at anything, like a board game or activity, I would flip out. If I lost anything, I considered myself a failure, similar to my drawings. So, Dr. Gay told my parents to help me practice losing. There was a certain game I enjoyed playing called the Memory Game. Y'know, where you flip over the cards one at a time, and if it matches, you get that pair? I never lost at that. So Mom went first, to try to get me to lose. But every game she played, SHE lost, and I won. Mom eventually gave up and told Dad to try and beat me. Even still I won every game. My parents reported this back to Dr. Gay. This trait didn't carry over, though, because I'm fine about losing any game now. Though sometimes I'll stop playing a game when I'm on a lucky streak, so I don't get disappointed from losing another game.

Aspies have a good memory. Well, I do at least. Aspies also are very determined, focused, but sometimes obsessive compulsive. Companies can take advantage of this, because they LOVE hiring employees with

Asperger's. They come in to work at time, get to work, and leave on time. They will be extremely focused on work and nothing else. The reason that my parents lost so many of those memory games was because they were thinking about bills, the laundry, dinner, etc. On the other hand, I was focused on one thing: Winning that memory game. Aspies don't get distracted easily. If they want to get something done, they won't stop or move until they've done so. If an aspie is working, they'll stay working possibly even through lunch because they need to get their work done. They won't be distracted with texting, or phones, or social media. I don't like texting, so it never distracts me. Ever. The point is, companies can take advantage of an aspie's valuable traits.

While I'm on the subject of things I don't like, let me say this: I've never liked sports. Ever since I was little, I just never got into them. My parents never made me enroll in any sports, so I never played them. I'm not a very athletic kid; I'm more of a brainy kid. Even if I tried to play sports now, I probably just wouldn't get the hang of it. In fact, I partially avoided sports back then because I thought I would get hurt or get angry.

I'd like to share a couple of things with ya. First, I loved numbers back then. I still like them now. But what I really liked were calculators. Or, as I called them, 'countulators'. You have to admit, that name makes a little more sense. That's why I called calculators that. If I wasn't drawing in daycare, I was probably on a calculator, adding and subtracting random numbers. I carried a calculator with me everywhere. I'd use it all the time and I'd even sleep with one next to me on my bed. Yes, I really loved those 'countulators'.

Second, whenever I would get in trouble, I didn't get spanked. Instead, I got a time out. I'd usually have to sit next to the wall for several minutes, and then apologize for what I may have done. One day, my mom received a little toy clock as a gift from one of her friends. It was a time out clock used to keep the time. It had a face, and when you set the clock, it would turn into a frown. As time went on, its face slowly turned into a smile. And when time was finally up, the clock would be smiling and it would make a loud ringing noise. I did not like this clock. The first time my mom tried the clock for a time out, I sat against the wall screaming and crying. I was scared of it. After that time, my mom never used the clock again. She even sent it back to her friend.

One of the things I hated the most about it was how loud it was. Loud noises have always been really stimulating for me. I don't think I would enjoy going to a concert because of how utterly loud it would be. Ergo, I've never gone to one. If I ever get stimulated by loud noises, I need to go somewhere quiet for a while and cool off. One of the LOUDEST places for me is the school cafeteria. With all of the kids in there yelling over each other, throwing food, and just being obnoxious, the cafeteria is one of the most stressful rooms in the school when in full use. So, I don't eat lunch in there. Instead, I bring my own lunch every day and I eat in a small, quiet room with some of my acquaintances. I prefer eating in there a lot more than eating in the cafeteria.

I developed a liking to rocks during this time. More specifically, crystals. There were many pebbles on the playground at daycare, because it made up the entire "floor". I would inspect these pebbles to find the ones that had crystals. If I found a crystal that I really liked, I would take it home and put it in a big bin full of rocks and crystals that I liked. I liked to talk to my friends, about those rocks, but I didn't have very many. I had a few friends, but only one really became a very good friend.

During my time in daycare I met one of my best friends: Zachary. Zachary and I met when we were both around four years old. We would hang out together, but since I had never really made a friend before, I did odd things. Whenever Zach would come to my house, we would play with trains. It was during one visit when I got mad at Zach and I threw a train at his head. There was another instance where Zach and I were swimming in the kiddy pool at our local swimming pool. One of Zach's parents was talking with my mom, and all of the sudden, I was dunking Zach in the water. I was angry for a reason I don't remember, but Zach put up with it every time. Today, both Zach and I are thirteen years old, and we're both 5' 7". Whenever he comes over, we play video games, board games, and sometimes wrestle. We both get along very well, and we make each other laugh a lot. I appreciate Zach for sticking with me all these years, and he's one of my best friends who really understands my challenges.

7 Elementary School

When I was five years old, I finally moved to my first public school. I was moving into kindergarten, and I was really freaking out about it because of all the change happening at once. I met a few kids in my class, some of whom I would still know years later. My kindergarten teacher struck me as a little odd. It seemed as if whenever I said something, she would turn around and glare at me for a couple of seconds. Kindergarten was extremely difficult for everyone. I still couldn't control myself, so I had a lot of meltdowns and got sent to the principal's office at least twice a week. I would hide under desks, throw things, yell at people, knock over desks and chairs, throw myself on the ground kicking and screaming, etc. This wasn't completely my fault. I was struggling with Asperger's, and since I was only five years old, I had next to NO time to work on my challenges. When I say meltdown, I don't mean tantrum. I mean kind of a breakdown because I was confused about what was happening and maybe I didn't know what I was feeling. There was a SPED team there, but they weren't trained to work with my challenges. The custodians even put a big refrigerator box in the room with a weighted blanket for me when I became overwhelmed. I could go into the refrigerator box and sit there until I calmed down. It was a safe place for me and had my stuffed animal and blanket. (To be clear, the refrigerator box is the big, cardboard box that the fridge comes in.)

Mom would talk to my teachers about my behavior, and it always angered her when teachers said this: "Well, he's just so smart; he should know better." No, that's not it. There's no correlation or causation between intellect and social awareness. You could have an IQ of 170 and still have immense trouble interacting with other people.

In the middle of my kindergarten year, my parents told me I was going to switch teachers because of the trouble I was having in that class. I moved to a different teacher's class, who I like a lot more. She was kind, understanding, and she taught me a lot that year. Of course, there were still many challenges I had to work through, but kindergarten was easier from then on.

When I moved to first grade, I had an even harder time. I hadn't progressed a lot in controlling my anger, so I was still hiding under desks, yelling at teachers, throwing objects, knocking over chairs and desks, and sometimes even destroying utensils. In fact, my anger had gotten to the point where I would become so angry that I would destroy the whole classroom. The teacher had to evacuate the students from the room, and they waited outside the room while I messed stuff up. I remember that on the first day everyone got juice boxes handed out by the principal, but that was pretty much the best day of first grade I can remember. My teacher barely understood me at all, which only brought more problems. My parents even brought little goodies that the teacher taped the whiteboard. If I didn't have a meltdown that day I would get the goodie. It was an incentive to behave. They didn't realize it wasn't that easy for me. (Every day I had to carry a big, heavy bin of books down to a nearby room to relieve stress. I enjoyed doing this, but I didn't like how heavy it was.) The teacher and I didn't get along very well. We would get in a lot of arguments, which led to me being sent down to the principal's office. One such argument went like this: it was reading time, and the teacher told everyone to go to the library in the room, or the reading corner. The room's "library" was only a small bookshelf with a couple of bean-bag chairs. To me, this wasn't a library. And to make matters worse, it wasn't really even in the corner. Madness, right? So I felt like I needed to address this to the teacher immediately. I said that it wasn't a library OR a corner, and the teacher said, "Well, that's what we're going to call it today." I made my rebuttal with, "Are you lying or are you just stupid?"

I wasn't the most charming kid back then. Needless to say, I was sent down to the principal's office. Not all of the power struggles that took place were my fault. The teacher was partially to blame for the way she worked with me. The social skills program still wasn't all that helpful, so first grade, in conclusion, was probably my worst year in elementary school.

An example of a power struggle that the teacher and I had was one day during recess. I spent recess walking around the playground all alone looking for the perfect stick. I had found a stick outside that I grew a particular liking to. I liked it so much, in fact, that I tried to bring it inside after recess. However, the teacher saw this stick and forbade me from coming inside until I got rid of the stick. But I really liked the stick, and insisted that I come inside with it. After the teacher said no again, I refused to come inside until they let me bring the stick in. The situation escalated to the point where the Principle was called out to help. After the incident took place, my parents had a meeting with the teacher, and they agreed to let me bring in sticks, as long as I left it on the filing cabinet until it was time to go home.

    Around this time, my parents were looking for special programs that helped children with their social skills, and they came across a program named Inspire Behavior. Inspire was run by a woman named Jennifer Kaut, and she was almost the only person there. The first day I went there, I was with my Mom, walking with Mrs. Jennifer. Mrs. Jennifer was explaining to us how they used equine therapy, or horse therapy, to help children. She talked about how horses are like humans: they don't want to be near a hyper or angry person, and are more attracted to calm and cool people. They can sense kids with challenges. Mom wasn't buying all of this at first. All three of us were walking around the fenced area where the horses were kept, and we noticed one horse in particular was following us. We didn't know who it was following, so we all stopped. The horse came over to me and nibbled my hair from over the fence. I said, "I think it likes me," and Mom started considering that this might all be true.

Mrs. Jennifer was, and is, a very knowledgeable woman on autism. She used to come to my AARD meetings for school, and she helped tremendously. But, one of the most important things she said was, "There is a function to the behavior." This means that there's a reason behind everything someone does, even if they have autism. This states that when it may seem like I'm doing something for no reason, I'm actually doing it for a reason.

One thing I did a lot was swear at the top of my lungs. However, it would only be if I was escalating, or if I was in an escalating situation. I would speak the foulest word I knew, and I would say it loudly over and over again. I always had to be removed from class, and I would be taken to the principal's office. At first, no one knew why I did this. Some thought I was just a rotten kid. However, they soon realized that I was probably swearing like that to get myself out of the room. There's a function to the behavior, so there was a reason I was swearing. I was smart enough to know that I needed to leave the room when I got upset, but I just didn't know how to get myself out. I thought, "Hey, swearing will definitely get me out of here," and that's what I did. It got me out every time.

Mrs. Jennifer was a very vital woman in my life growing up, and I wouldn't be as better off as I am now without her. In fact, one of the main reasons I'm so much better socially is because I went to interventions early in life. I learned how to get better with my social interactions when I was young, and places like Inspire Behavior helped me a lot. Mrs. Jennifer now isn't the only person running Inspire Behavior; there are MANY more employees, and the company has grown exponentially! Mrs. Jennifer now travels the world speaking about autism, and I'm glad she helped me.

One more program that helped me was the Autism Project at the University of Texas. What they did was they had their students who were studying autism and pair them up with kids on the Autism spectrum. This let the students learn more about autism up close and from a child who actually had autism. The University of Texas had a grant that let them work with kids on the Autism spectrum, and they held events like sleepover parties, where the kids can sleep over at the University of Texas. This was important because it gave the kids, and me, the experience of sleeping away from home for the first time: something I didn't get to do before, since I was dealing with social challenges and emotional anxiety. So I also thank the University of Texas for holding events like that, as it can help children like me with their struggles and anxiety.

While I was in early elementary, I was still going to daycare, but only for afterschool care. I met many different kids in afterschool care, but there was one thing that stood out about after-school care. It was unstructured. That's the key word here today: Un. Structured.

I was a very organized little boy. I'm still quite organized today. Back then, and even now, I can't stand leaving certain things untidy. If something unstructured catches my eye, I will WANT to fix it. The reason behind this was because I had Asperger's, and some aspies are very structured. That, and I was a perfectionist, and I still am today. But that's beside the point. Afterschool care was a combination of all different grades, from first to sixth. Ergo, there were many different kids of all ages in afterschool care. All of these kids gathered in a gym that was being built while I was still younger. I even remember the days it was being built. Inside the gym was sort of chaos. There was a lot going on, and I was overwhelmed quickly. There were kids everywhere, and the teachers never did a whole lot. There was virtually no schedule.

(Speaking of schedules, schedules are really helpful for me, and they definitely would've helped me more in afterschool care. I don't use too many schedules now, but it's something I admit I should have in my life again. It gives me a sense of structure, and lets me know that nothing is going to be different that day. If something happens at school where the schedule for classes is rearranged, I have to know everything before I leave anywhere. I have to know where to

go, what time classes let out, etc. If I don't know, I'll start freaking out, so a schedule is very important for me in school.)

A good portion of the boys there were a lot older than me. I remember that they would occupy the air hockey table, the foosball table, and even the basketball court. (I started getting into shooting hoops, and I once even recorded the amount of basketball shots I had made at daycare through one summer: by memory!) One of these boys was, say, 5 years older than me, and he liked to pick on me. He would usually call me "dork", and just make fun of me. One recess, I was climbing the playscape, and he was standing by the slide. He said, "What's up, dork?" I ran over to a teacher and told them that he had called me a dork. They said that if he called me a dork again, he'd be getting time-out. I ran back over to the boy and told him what the teachers told me. His rebuttal was, "Alright, dork." So I RAN back over to the teacher and told them that he had called me a dork again. The boy was sent to time-out for the rest or recess. (Eventually, after years of torment, the boy decided to apologize to me about his behavior, which I accepted.)

I was sometimes picked on by everybody for my personality, though. One day, a group of boys began to throw pebbles at me at recess. When word got to my mom, she decided to take me out of after-school care. She knew the place was unstructured, but this was the last straw. After my transition, my dad had to change jobs to fit his time schedule with picking me up after school.

(Parents: when you have a child with autism, it is not rare for one of the parents to have to change their job to fit their child's schedule.)

When I moved to second grade, things changed rather quickly. It was only around 26 days in when I was told that I was moving to a different school. The current school was not working for me since they didn't have a specific program for behavior challenges, and my parents said they had found a better school near us with a social skills team to help me at the new school I was moving to. I stayed at the first school for about ten more days, and I moved to the other school the next day. My family and I had toured the school before I moved there, so nothing was strikingly overwhelming. I knew absolutely nobody there, so making friends was hard for me. Second grade wasn't really that eventful. I had a really nice teacher who I

got along with, and I made a few acquaintances. I stayed in that class for the rest of that year.
However.

There was a huge part in my life that I believed happened around this time. All my life I had wanted a brother. I was born an only child, so when I saw someone with a sibling, I would become rather jealous. My parents had been working on adopting a younger brother, and we came across a child named Jon. Jon was a month older than I was, but he acted like the little brother. He had behavioral issues that were much worse than mine at the time, and possibly even worse than I ever had at any time in my life. He would CONSTANTLY throw fits, scream, and use inappropriate behavior. When Jon and I would wrestle, it would ALWAYS end with him crying, and he would even bite me on occasion. There were some times when we would get along, but not very often. There were COUNTLESS occasions when he had a meltdown in public, including the grocery store and at a waterpark. When Mom, Jon and I were at the grocery store once, Jon said he wanted a certain product, and Mom said no. He almost immediately threw himself on the floor in the middle of one of the isles. He just lay there, waiting for us to cave in, but we didn't. After a notable amount of time, Jon got up and ran all the way down the aisle next to him, even scaring off a couple of people. Another occasion was when Jon and I were at a waterpark, and our parents said that we had two more minutes before we had to leave. Jon thought they said we had to go, so he refused to leave. When it was time to go, he sat in the corner of the small park, refusing to get up. Dad had to go in there and CHASE him back and forth until he caught Jon. When we got into the car, Mom was furious with Jon, and said that he was NEVER going back to that waterpark ever again. After this incident, Mom and Dad decided that Jon wasn't a good fit for our family. It was a few months later that he left our family, and I was back to where I started. It was soon after this that I decided I wanted a big brother, and we began our search again.

Back to school stuff now. Hold on a sec. What about the whole reason I moved to that new school in the first place? It was about that social skills group, right? Yes, it was. The group was a team of people that helped students with behavioral challenges who could help WAY more. A random person from the team would check on various students in their classes to see how they were doing. If a student was having a hard time in class, the teacher could request someone from the team to take them down to the main room. The main room was mostly a place for students to cool off, whether they were just getting a little stressed or if they NEEDED to be down there because of how angry they were. If a student was having a complete meltdown, the student would be put in a medium-small sized room with nothing in the room. There were four walls with a door that were hard and completely white, so the student couldn't break anything. If the students got ahold of a pencil, they would sometimes write on the wall. If a student needed to get work done, the team would put a desk in there and give the students their work. When a student has cooled off, someone from the team would open the door and ask if they were ready to come out. If they were, then great. If they weren't, they'd stay in there. If they pretended to be ready, they would soon be put back in. As barbarian this tactic might seem, it really did help. The team really helped me improve my behavior over time, and they're one of the main reasons I am who I am today.

Okay, so back to the story. When I moved to third grade, things actually started happening. I became extremely anxious to go to school, because I was always afraid I was going to throw up. I hated throwing up. Even thinking about it made me anxious. Every day, the anxiety of going to school made me feel slightly queasy, and I always thought I was going to be sick. To counteract this, each week my mom sent me with gum, and left a six pack of lemon lime soda in the nurse's office for if I ever got anxious. The soda was carbonated, so it made my stomach feel better, and the gum was for me to chew on when I got worked up. For as long as I can remember, my parents always gave me something chewy and sweet at times, like candy. They gave me it because the chewing relieved my stress.

During that year, I had become interested in a line of collectible toys. I was almost obsessed with the toy, too. I always wanted to go to the store to buy more of them. Soon after third grade began, I was asking the students in my class if they had heard or liked the toy. I came across one kid who collected them like I did, and we soon started to hang out together. His name was Shane. We would talk about the toy, but usually just make ourselves laugh. Unfortunately, the teacher didn't appreciate the noise we made. My third grade teacher was out there. I sort of liked her, but I held a grudge against her, because she always tried to separate me from Shane. I don't blame her, though. Whenever Shane and I talked, we would end up making a lot of noise. Shane was very rowdy, and he would be loud at times. He also swore a fair amount, which I didn't approve. Regardless, we got along and made each other laugh. One of our best times to talk was during reading time, when everyone found a spot to read a book that they might have brought. We wouldn't always read; instead, we would just talk. So, the teacher always tried to separate us during that time.

The thing I remember most about this year was something I didn't quite plan on. Ever since I had become friends with Shane, I started bringing some of the toys I was into to school. I would pick the ones I wanted to bring and put them in a small, plastic bag to show to Shane. He would do the same, but we rarely actually traded. It was soon when some of the students in my class became interested in what Shane and I brought to school. Soon, THEY started getting into the toy, and sometimes brought their own. It was only a matter of time before the toy was the talk of the "town". I don't know if only MY class was into them, but it felt like the entire third grade was into them. On most days I would bring one toy, and I would place it on my desk. It was one day when I returned to find the toy I brought was gone. I think someone might have taken it, but I don't think I ever recovered it. (It didn't matter, though, because I ended up getting the same one at the store soon after.) There were actually multiple occasions when I almost lost some of the toys I brought. The best time for me to play with my toys with everyone was at recess. There was one time when I threw one up in the air, and it got stuck in a tree. I recovered it the next day. There was another occasion where I buried one in the gravel, and I couldn't find it when our class had to go inside. The issue with this one was that it was from the next series of the toy that hadn't even COME OUT near us yet. I was the ONLY one in school who had it. After a lot of begging, the teacher allowed me to go outside with a member of the social skills team to find it, and thankfully, I did find it.

Not all of this was fun and games, though. I would tinker with the toys at my own time, usually when I needed to be focused on something else. There was one incident where I was playing with my toy while the teacher was reading a book at Reading Time. The teacher stopped, and waited for me to stop playing. We got into a minor verbal altercation, which left me irritated when school was let out. My dad always picked me up after school, and he always wore a cap that represented his job. When I walked outside, I saw a man in a hat that I thought was my dad. I had already planned out what I was going to do. I would throw my backpack to my dad, who would catch it and ask, "What's wrong?" I would respond by telling him what happened, and everything was going to be okay. When I walked up to the man in the cap, I threw my backpack to him, and he caught it. It was then when I looked up, only to find out it was, in fact, NOT my dad who I just threw my backpack at. He looked down at me, and he asked, "And you threw this at me because?" I responded with, "Sorry, sorry, sorry, I thought you were someone else."

He said I was fine, but I'm still a little embarrassed about it today.

There was one day at recess when I saw a group of kids throwing small rocks at a big rock in the ground. Having been obsessed with rocks and crystals when I was younger, I went over to find out what they were doing. They said they were trying to break the rocks open to see what was inside. I had always been interested in rocks, so I joined them in their expedition. Somedays I found good rocks, other days nothing showed, but there was one girl I met who I soon became friends with. She also liked the rock game, but we soon started talking as friends. There was a boy in my class who I was "frienemies" with, and the girl and I would 'tough him out' whenever he came by to smite us. That boy and I sometimes hung out, but other times we hated each other's guts. Looking back on it now, there were some occasions where I admit that I bullied him, and I regret doing that.

Now, there is one thing from this year that I remember a lot, and not for a good reason. I had my grandma and grandpa at the time, who lived 60 miles away from us, and we would visit them on holidays, such as

Thanksgiving Christmas, Spring Break, and Summer Break. Everyone in the family called them Mamaw and Papaw. Mamaw is a little, sweet, religious woman who everyone loves. Papaw was a very tall, "rough" man, who liked to goof around. Whenever I was sitting on a certain spot on the couch, he'd say, "You're in my seat, buster," and we'd pretend wrestle for the spot. I love them both very much.

It was April 19, Papaw's birthday, and I was watching videos on my computer. I started to hear a noise coming from my parents' bedroom. I had headphones on, so I couldn't tell if it was laughing or crying. After I waited a while, I found out someone was crying. I walked slowly over to the bedroom, and I knocked on the door. My dad opened the door, and I heard that my Mom was weeping heavily. I asked what had happened, and Dad was reluctant to tell me. He told me to leave, but I was resistant. I asked what had happened again, and he told me, "Papaw died." I have no idea how this was all I managed to say, but all I said was, "...Dang." I had never dealt with a death in the family before, so I didn't know how to feel. Papaw was a former smoker; he had smoked for over twenty years, and had quit for ten years. Eventually the years of smoking had caught up to him, coincidently on his birthday. Everyone was sending text messages saying, "Happy birthday!" but he wasn't replying. Everyone started saying, "This isn't like him," and investigated further. It turns out that he died of a heart attack in his hotel room. He was a working man, so he wasn't always home. We immediately left for Mamaw's house, where everyone had come to mourn. There was a 'ceremony' where we celebrated Papaw's life. Whenever Mom cried, I would wipe her tears away. There was also a funeral, but I didn't go to that one. The whole time I never cried once, and I don't know how I did that.

Sometimes I still feel astonished that Papaw is really gone. Mamaw is still alive today, but she is getting old. We visit her more often, because she lives there all by herself, and she gets lonely. I am thankful she is still around, though.

As third grade ended, my parents told me that the social skills group that helped me through second and third grade was moving to another school. I asked what school it was, and they told me that it was my old school. The team was moving to my old school. So, I had to move with them. This meant that I could see my old friends again. I was going back.

During this time, my family and I were still searching for an older brother, and we found a boy named Jacob. He was three years older than me. We thought he might be a good match, so  we went to visit him at his foster home. We went to the nearest arcade, and decided to let him stay with us at our house for a while. After about one year of him at our house, we adopted Jacob, and he's still with us now. I couldn't be more thankful that he's my brother. My mom said that I was just beaming on the day of the adoption. Jacob's helped me a lot over the years, like reminding me when I should change my tone of voice, and teaching me all about the Xbox 360.

When I moved to fourth grade, not much happened. It was cool to see my old school and my old friends again, but not too much new happened. As the year went on, I learned how to control myself even better, thanks to the team. But, I also had a really good teacher. From first grade and beyond, I hated to write. I hated it. I thought I would embarrass myself with my awful writing, so I said I hated it. My teacher helped me overcome that gap, and she's one of the main reason's I'm able to write this book. Thanks to her, I have realized that I don't really hate writing.

One of the most important things to note is that I had two ways of calming myself down. I chewed gum, and I drew. I loved to draw. I would draw pictures of random things, or, most of the time, I would draw stickmen comics. That's what I loved to draw. Doing this helped me calm down, and it diverted my attention away from my worries. I was given "drawing time" as a reward for good behavior in class. But yes, I loved to draw. Unfortunately, not so much anymore. I think that my drawing isn't QUITE what it used to be, and I think I would just embarrass myself. Anyway, as I said earlier, not much happened in fourth grade. However, fifth grade had more to offer.

When I moved into fifth grade, things were very rough. I had a teacher I didn't like very much, and I knew no one in the class, which was the main issue. None of my friends were in my classes, so I felt lonely. At recess, I would usually walk around the border of the playground, and nothing else. I would usually come in the classroom early to arrange seats, and that helped to ease anxiety, but I was desperate to find friends. One day, I noticed that there was a group of boys in my class who often hung out together. I analyzed them when they would hang out. I thought that I could probably be friends with them. But, one thing I noticed about them was that they were quite rowdy. They would make odd noises and sometimes get in trouble. Regardless, they made me laugh. I realized that if I wanted to become friends with them, I would have to do what they did. I knew it would be hard for me to do that, but I was desperate for a friend and would do almost anything. Eventually, I sat with one of the boys at lunch one day, and we talked to each other. His name was Lucas. Whenever we talked, we would usually talk about rather absurd things, and we only got to talk at lunch, because we didn't sit near each other. That would soon change. One thing our teacher did was rearrange the classroom seats every once in a while. It just so happened that Lucas and I ended up at the same table. We got to talk a lot more there, and we soon became acquaintances. I was getting somewhere. One day at lunch, Lucas invited me to sit with the guys. (I don't recall this moment to perfection, but I believe that is what happened.) So I sat down with Lucas, and I met the three other kids who made up the group: Stan, Joe, and Al.

    Stan and Lucas had been friends for a long time, so they were the ones who got along the best. Joe had to move before the second semester even began, so he wasn't around, and Al was the one who made everyone laugh. Before long, I had become acquaintances with Stan and Lucas. At lunch and recess, we would talk, but mostly mess around. Their sense of humor was fairly foreign to me, and it was a loud one at that. But, I did what I had to. This did come at a price, though. I would usually get in trouble for the noise I made whenever I would try to make the guys laugh. Stan and Lucas somehow miraculously avoided getting in trouble; it was almost always just me. Regardless, Stan, Lucas and I still hung out.

I have always been a rule-follower, as most aspies are. I follow the rules that I think are right. If someone's fighting, break them up and try to make things right. At least, that's what I thought when I got into my first "fight" at school. Somewhere within the school year, I came across a physical altercation on the school campus. Two boys were fake-fighting, and I knew both of them, though not personally. Being the rule-follower I was, I decided to step in between the two boys and tell them to break it up. To my surprise, they started fake-punching me. Their fists made contact with my face, but it didn't hurt in the slightest, as there was no force put into the blows. Before

I knew it, I had gotten involved in the fight myself, and I soon put one of the boys in a choke-hold. This choke-hold was real, and he punched my stomach to get me to let go. The punch didn't hurt, but it was at this moment I realized I had gone far enough. I immediately let go and backed away with my hands in the air. Though the boy was calling me an idiot, it didn't affect me, and I walked to my dad's car, where he picks me up to go home. I learned a lesson that day. Even though I was a rule follower, I needed to realize what exactly is okay for me to get involved in. Trying to break up a fight by myself was not a good idea, and I should have gotten and administrator to break up the fight. Still, most kids with Asperger's are rule-followers, and this incident shows that I was a rule-follower myself.

My teacher for the year was questionable. She was strict, and it felt almost as if she targeted me. There was one instance where we had a substitute teacher, and the boys and I were talking. We were getting loud, so the teacher came over to talk to us. On the other hand, the table next to us was beginning to act up. While the teacher was talking to us, a boy from the other table had stood up on the table and began jumping around like a chimpanzee. I told the teacher about them, but she told me she was worrying about us, not them.

After a good amount of discomfort throughout the year, I eventually asked to hold a meeting after school. My parents asked if I wanted them to attend the meeting but I said "No". The teacher, principal, and social skills team came, and we had a good talk about what I felt. I talked about my discipline, and the discipline of others. I think the adults were fairly surprised that I called a meeting, and I might have opened the eyes of some. There was even a point where I started to break up emotionally and the principal asked if I needed my dad, who was waiting outside, I said, "No, I'm fine. Let's keep going." Not a huge amount was changed after that meeting, but I think it was just a good meeting to have. Before the year ended, I learned how to contact Stan, and we still talk today. I haven't seen him in person for almost two years, but we still keep in touch.

Like I said before, the reason I'm so well-mannered today is because I had early interventions. I got help when I was young. One thing I've always hated was singing. I HATE SINGING. I also hate dancing. I HATE DANCING. I think singing and dancing make me look foolish, so I refrain from embarrassing myself. Ever since I was little I hated music class. I thought the kids in music class were so irritating, what with their singing off key, bad instrument playing, etc. But I especially hated it when they sang. I thought it was childish, and I did not want to be associated with such an immature practice, nor the ones singing. I thought that it was, yes, embarrassing.

  As I grew older, I still didn't like music class. I usually walked back and forth in the side or hallway of the room. But, I would still refuse to participate with what they were doing. In fact, ANYTHING that I think would be embarrassing I will completely refuse to do. My accommodations at school allowed me to sit outside of the music room door if I was overwhelmed. However, during the end of the year in fifth grade, my music teacher told the class that we would practice playing the recorder. You had a set amount of songs to practice, and anyone who plays a song right will earn a colored piece of yarn to tie around your recorder. Each song had their own color, and they were arranged in the order you earn colored belts in karate classes, with each song increasing in difficulty as you move along. At first, I didn't want to participate. I thought I would embarrass myself with my awful recorder skills. I also could barely stand being in the room because of the horrendous noise. It sounded just like how you would expect a room full of fifth-graders playing recorders to sound. (In case you don't know, a recorder is kind of like a flute.) However, Mom and Dad urged me to at least try. They didn't want me to be uncomfortable in music class, but they still wanted me to be exposed to the world of music. So, I told them that I would try playing the recorder, but only as long as I got to do it in the Achieve room. (Achieve was the social skills group that helped me through second to fifth grade.) So, I started practicing the recorder in the Achieve room, and as I played it more I began to like it. I soon got the hang of playing and realized that I was ahead of all my classmates. As I became more comfortable playing the recorder, I decided it would be okay if I started practicing in the music room. Before long, I had completed around eight songs, and I only had one more song left, when no one else had even gotten past four songs. It was just a few days before summer when I completed the final song and earned the final belt: the black belt. Only one other person in the whole school had earned a black belt. So, for just trying out one thing, I turned out surpassing everyone in the school at it. I even started taking piano lessons after learning the recorder. Just goes to show that some things are worth a shot. If you don't take a chance, you might miss out on what could have been a winning situation.

8 Middle School

When I moved into sixth grade, I was moving into middle school. Since I was moving into middle school, I thought I was going to die. From what I knew, I thought the bigger kids there would try to kill sixth graders like me. Plus, the new system would drive me nuts. I would have to get used to a new schedule, a new school, new kids, etc. But after the first day, I was fine, and I learned that middle school wasn't that bad. The past social skills team didn't move with me, so I had a new team, which I was almost the most worried about. As it turns out, the people are really nice and supportive, and they never yell at me.

(Parents: I sometimes stress out over starting a new year at school, and it helps me a lot to meet the teachers I'm going to have that year before the new school year starts. I've done this since elementary school, and it helps with my anxiety and gets me ready for change.)

New kids? Yeah, let me tell ya. I'm currently in eighth grade, reflecting onto sixth grade. Here's what middle school essentially is. Middle school is this tiny building where kids from all over town are going through puberty: they're trying to figure out who they are, what they want to do in life, as well as trying to understand their emotions; and these kids are all shoved into this tiny hole called middle school. It's pretty much why people consider middle school the worst school years ever. They're going through puberty, and all the while they have to deal with others going through the same thing. It's not fun.

To give you my perspective about middle school, it's exhausting. Not to toot my own horn here, but I'm much more mature than half of the kids in my school, and it's really tiring to put up with others around me.

Middle school is full of the typical teenagers. These are the kids who think they're all that. They think they're sooo pretty and perfect and important. They spend every second on their phones, even in class, taking selfies and posting them on their social media pages and crap. Query: Why the heck would you need all of those photos of yourself, much less need to take them in the first place? What are you going to do, frame them in your house? Yeah, THAT'LL make you look good. Not only that, but they talk back to teachers as if they have authority over them! The teacher tells them to stop talking, and the reply by saying they never spoke, when in reality they had been talking before. They're so noisy. They NEVER stop talking! They're so rude to everyone for almost no reason. They talk to you like you're less than them! They act like idiots! They don't think about consequences to their actions, and if they get in trouble, they need to throw a fit. If they're gonna get kicked out of the classroom, then they're going out with a bang. Or, they'll divert the class' attention away from them and towards a funny comment they make, such as blurting out a swear word right before the door shuts behind them, so that everyone will be focused on the word that person just said rather than how stupid that person just made themselves look. They'll say they don't care if they get a referral just so they can show the class how tough and rebellious they are. Well, I'm not buying it. I'm not buying ANY of it! I don't think they're ALL idiots, but I'm convinced that many of them really are. They act dumb enough to where I believe they really are. They most likely act this way because they think that they can be accepted by their "friends" if they do what their friends do. They think that if they act rude to everybody then they can fit in. Those are called "followers". I'm not a follower. **I don't need to fit in. I don't need to be part of the latest trend. I know who I am.** Some of these people can't get enough of THEMSELVES. They get wrapped up in their own ego and fail to fully realize the world around them. They're stuck in this fantasy where they're so important and everyone loves them and cares about everything they have to say. They post pictures of themselves standing in front of mirrors looking either buff with their shirt off wearing a cap or posing with ten buckets of makeup on their face. Then, they say things like "I woke up like this," or "no filter," when they have all this crap on their face. You can call me a "hater", but take a minute to look at yourself. No, actually, take a minute to look at anything BUT yourself! Put your phone up and have a REAL experience of life! Quit looking at the world through your phones, and quit expecting everyone to care about how pretty or buff you are! We're all just people! How can anyone think this is okay?! It's asinine!! To sum it up, the current youth of millennials, teenagers, and young adults have an inflated ego and are detached from the world around them. And frankly, it's heart-breaking. To think that these people are going to be the ones controlling the world someday. How is anything going to get better when these people don't try to better themselves?? Maybe I'm part of the problem. Maybe I'm really no different from them, and I'm just one of those "haters". But one thing's for sure. I don't use social media at the moment I'm writing this, and for at least one person out there, I've said what they've been thinking. I'll say this again: I don't need to take countless photos of myself to like myself, and I don't need to wear any foolish makeup to find out who I am. I don't need to wear the best new shoes or the coolest new apparel to be accepted by my friends. I know who I am, and I don't need nor want that kind of lifestyle. I follow my own rule: the key to being yourself is by not trying to be anybody else. This is merely a trend and I don't need to involve myself in it. Oh, you just put a picture of yourself online? I couldn't care less if you're pretty. The only thing attractive to me is knowledge. I value if you're smart over how you look. If I find out that you don't know how to spell the word "you're", that's a deal-breaker. I learned that in first grade. How can anyone manage to mess that up? Especially now that they're in eighth grade! It still feels like I'm walking around campus with a bunch of kindergartners. Seriously, the students act like they're in kindergarten. If you act like you're stupid, I'll assume that you are stupid. If you're not stupid, then stop acting like you're stupid. It's as simple as that!

But back to the FOCUS team: Sometimes I can have conversations with them, and when I get angry, they just let me cool off, and then they talk to me in a calm tone. I couldn't really ask for anything else from them. I find the school's cafeteria to be overstimulating, so I go down to their main office to eat. There are also other kids in the team that eat down there. Their room serves as a place to calm down, and we even get to play video games. They really are a great team, and they've helped me a lot over the past two years. Not a whole lot happened in sixth grade; it was just new to me. Surprisingly, it was probably my best year ever. But, things were about to change. A lot.

9 The Stairs Collapse

Now that I've caught up to the near present, let me say something. The reason I don't include seventh grade in Every Day's a Staircase is because that year defines this whole chapter. It's the year that my entire thought process changed, and with that, my life. It's the year when the stairs collapsed, which left me stuck from moving on. It was one of the hardest years of my life. So, here's the story of seventh grade.

In the summer of 2014, I hit adolescence, or puberty. A whole new set of hormones started to flow through my body, and I was a little overwhelmed by it. Acne grew on my face, I began to grow facial hair, underarm hair, and... well... THAT hair. But most of all, I became depressed. There was not a lot to do around the house, so I became rather bored, and with this boredom came time to think. Time to think very deeply about things that I may not like to think about. I usually stayed holed up in my room, which didn't help anything. As you could imagine, starting school again would be hard.

So, when I moved into seventh grade, things got difficult. Firstly, I had none of my friends in ANY of my classes, so I was basically alone. Secondly, I was going through puberty, and thirdly, most of the classes were quite boring and hard to get into. When the classes were boring, I would stand up and pace around the classroom. During this pacing, I would think about things that I wanted to think about. Sometimes if I really wanted to keep thinking about something, and I couldn't sit still, I would need to get up and walk around. It was fine with the teachers, because they knew I needed to do that. Pacing in class is another accommodation I have in school. Sometimes, though, this would get out of hand.

This only happened at home. I would be thinking about something, and I would get very deep into it. I would then start thinking about it in a bad way, and I couldn't get out of it. This is what I call Spiraling. When I spiral, I can't get out of it easily, and I really hate being in it. It's called a spiral because the thoughts spiral downwards, and the thoughts go back and forth, creating a void of depression. The only way to stop is to think about it until I find a good place to stop. Only then can I stop.

I have my own way of dealing with perseveration, but it's a little complicated. First, I identify the problem. "What exactly am I thinking about? What's the issue that I want to go over here?" In order to find this subject, I rewind the moment or memory over and over again until I find the answer I think fits. Then I ask myself: "How can I fix this?" If I think there is a way to fix it, I start thinking about the memory a little more. If I don't think there is a way to fix it, I move on to the next question: "Is it worth worrying about?" Here I come to the simple and quick solution: yes, or no, and why. I think about the memory one last time and decide: Is it worth thinking about? Then I decide: "No, I just don't need to think about it because it won't get me anywhere right now." Then I move on. I usually pick "no" because it's perseveration. I don't want to perseverate. But, in a sense, the whole process to stop perseveration IS the perseveration. Meaning, the whole reason I perseverate is because I don't want it to go on any longer, so I try to perseverate as short as possible. This is the whole "thinking about it over and over" thing, but only for as long as I have to before I decide I should stop thinking about it. . I perseverate for the cause to stop perseveration. 'Told ya it was complicated.

(Parents: If your child spirals just like I do, and you don't know how to get them to stop, take their mind off of their own thoughts. Divert their attention; get their mind onto something else so they can stop thinking about bad things. Suggest that they play their video games, watch TV, read, go for a walk anything that they might enjoy and could get them to think about other things. I usually play video games when I spiral at home. I have a tablet that I use to watch videos, but I stay away from it when I start to spiral, as it is usually the thing that puts me in the spiral. I usually spiral when I watch too many videos and I catch myself on the tablet too long. So parents, if you have a child that spirals like I do, have them do something else to get their mind on that one thing.)

Anyway, to give you an idea of my spirals, here's the worst one that haunts me daily. When I get older; not when I grow up, but when I get older, I want to be a creator. Not a policeman, or a firefighter, not an astronaut, or even the president. I want to be a creator. I feel that a creator has as much if not more power than the people in charge. Creators can make things that convey emotions, thoughts, and feelings. They can create a story that can captivate the minds and hearts of anyone. They can create things so powerful that those creations can change the world, and even define and create a generation by itself. That's what I want to do. I want to create. For all of those reasons. Of course, everyone wants to change the world, and I'm no exception. But there is a huge issue for me. I have doubt. Doubt that I can do that.

What I feel is a combination of my hormones from puberty and my thoughts from my overly-analytical mind. But what I feel is that the time when I can change the world is so far from now. I'm just a kid, do I have to wait 20 years to be able to do anything? What could I do now? I'm thirteen years old. I have to wait, right? I don't want to. I want to do it now, so I can stop being tormented by my own stupid feelings.

When I talk about power in creations, I see this mostly in video games. Video games have really changed everything. It was barely even 35 years ago when they didn't even exist. Now, they've advanced so much, and evolved to the point where they have nearly taken over the earth. At first, it looked like a fad. People thought, "Ah, these kids today. It's just one of those things they do. It'll pass." But it didn't. Oh, no siree. That fad stuck around. It had a lot of business to take care of. And it still does. Who knows when its reign might end? When will the day come when it really does die out? What will we do then? Is it within my lifetime? What will I do? If the world could change so much in 35 years, what could happen in the next 35 years?

If you haven't figured it out already, I want to create video games. I see video game creators today and I think about them. They really seem to have it made. They get to create extremely influential things and get rightfully credited with changing the world. Their creations become larger than life and inspire people, inspire more things to happen. Inspire. What a strong word. Could I do that? Can I inspire people like creators do? Can I make something where people who like it can be considered fans? That's what I want. But I don't know. I want to inspire. But I'm just one person. What could I POSSIBLY do? It just seems so long from now. A long, long road where anything could happen. I could change the world in every way I want to, or something horrible could happen that would cripple my dreams. I'm afraid of the future. I just don't want anything bad to happen. But what if it does? Then what? What am I left to do? What is my purpose then?

Back to game developers. Behind the praise they work their butts off. Really. They're tired at the end of the day. They need to rest. Is it worth it? Am I cut out for it? Is the work worth the praise? Worse yet, is there praise? Are my feelings just an illusion of what the reality behind game developing is? It can't be, because I couldn't handle it. I've formed my opinions, I've felt the feelings. I can't give up now. Only to possibly have them crushed decades later? I really want to go through with this. I really want to change the world. But in a few years, what will change already? How can I create something that can spark a revolution, a new era in history? I don't know if I need to, but it feels like it. If you can think of any famous video game right now, do it. Got one? Yeah, I'm sure you do. Depends on who's reading this right now. I don't know if a young'un could get this far. Did you? I hope. Anyway, the video game that you thought of is probably a pretty old game, isn't it? That's the thing. When the video game fad was first beginning to grow, it was the perfect chance for the creators to jump in and make something. With these creations, they changed the world and created a new generation of people and memories. That's the kind of thing I want to do. I want to make a game that influential to a generation. Maybe not just a game, but an invention. A game console of some sort. But how can I make it any more special than the ones today? What can I invent? Discover? But most games today, they've lost hope. It's rehash after rehash until every game's the same game. Just with a different font and pictures on the cover. Even if a game developer HAS it done right, their effort gets lost in the sea of crud that people jump and drool over, never to be discovered for good. If it does get discovered, so what? It's never huge. You can know about it, but hardly anyone else will. That's not good enough for me. It feels that to make a really good, memorable, innovative, inspirational, influential and revolutionary creation or game, it has to be a very early adaptation of its concept. Take Mickey Mouse. You've heard of him, of course! Everyone has! He was created when animation was really just starting to be a big thing. Now take Pac-Man. You've heard of him, of course!

Everyone has! He was created when video games were really just starting to become a thing. So, can I do this? Maybe this could be my future: "Hey, have you heard of _____? Of course you have! Everyone has! Nicolas Saliani created _____ just when _____ games were starting to REALLY become a thing." What if my creation becomes big, but I don't like how it came out? I can't change it, so then what? Maybe I could make a new type of digital reality. Then make it into a game console, and then, games. A new concept. Then I create. Now everybody knows. I don't want it to be that convoluted, but I'm just so doubtful.

    Please don't get me wrong. I want to create for happiness. To give people something to remember and cherish. To give people something to follow and love. When people get down, they can think about my creations and feel better. They can create my creations again! Recreation! Recreation shows me that people really do appreciate my creations, and that's all I want. To know they love it. They can make art from my creations! They can make my music sound new! (I also want to make music for my games.) There's so much the people can do with my creations. I want my creations to be important to people and the world. But lots of creators make things for one purpose. Money.

I could honestly care less about the money. I know I need money to stay on my feet, but I would never be easy to sell out. In the case of a business offer, it would depend on what could happen aside from the money I get to really reel me in on a deal. But money, oh, it can be evil! Money has corrupted the minds of most big businesses today. They can sell out the quality of creations for money without batting an eyelash. I can't do that at all. I couldn't imagine myself being ABLE to do that. The point is even though people do this, their creations flourish. A lot. How can I compete? How can I stand out? Do good guys really finish last? How can I captivate the world? Wait for the powerful ones to die? No, that's irrational AND corrupted. The way things stand, video games as we know them TODAY don't have much time. Soon enough people will realize it's not what it used to be. I don't know when, but it can't be too long from now. It's already happening. Just very slowly. By the time I'm old enough to change something, will it be too late? Will the concept of video games and digital entertainment be a thing of the past? A memory? Just… a way things used to be…?

In the end, I'm my worst enemy. I'm the only one telling myself this, reminding me of the things that could happen. "Turn back now! Bad things will happen because YOU'RE NOT IMPORTANT!" And I need to get past myself. The biggest question is how. How? How can I do this? How can I get past now? How can I make sure my dreams come true? The worst part for me is that I think about this every day! EVERY DAY! I can't get away from it! It's impossible to escape, and I'm doomed to put myself in a depressing spiral almost every day of my life. It really, really sucks.

Sorry for the rambling, but I just needed to get that out. That's just how my mind can race sometimes. Ugh… I just wish I could ask them. The creators. The good ones. What was it like? Was it hard? What did you feel? How did you do it?...Was it worth it? If only I could ask. I'd feel so much better. Then again, I guess that would spoil the surprise. Maybe the future is something meant to be discovered and made, not known. I only wish the doubt could go away. One thing that I do know is that when I wake up in the morning, I feel better every time. I always do.

So yeah, that's one of my worst fears ever. Sorry if I droned on, but I was very tired the night I wrote that. Still, that doesn't mean I wasn't being truthful. Anyway, let me continue.

I was still depressed when I moved into seventh grade because I was going through puberty and I was trying to figure out who I was. I saw things I used to like in a whole different light, and compared them to my dreams of game design. This created trouble for me, putting myself into a spiral where I think about bad things over and over again. Some nights I cried because I thought nothing good would happen for me. It was those nights where I felt truly hopeless. To help me get through the rest of the year, we went to go see a man of my past once again: Dr. Gay.

Whenever we would go see Dr. Gay again, I just talked about what had been ailing me before, and we worked it out together. There weren't any real new "tactics" for me to try, but I went only to talk about my feelings with someone who wasn't my mom or dad, which I think helped.

Right before Christmas break, I came down with a case of the flu. Most of the time, I was in my parents' bedroom watching TV. I didn't feel good at all, and I ended up missing the entire last week of school for the first semester. My parents had made a doctor's appointment on a Monday to find out what sickness I had, because we just thought I had a cold. When the doctor stepped in the room, he proceeded to do the small check-up that all doctors do. He was in the middle of checking my adenoids when I slumped down in my chair, unconscious. The doctor then grabbed a trash can and pulled it in front of me for when I woke up. I gained consciousness again seconds later, when I felt like I needed to vomit. As if the doctor predicted it (It's likely he's seen this before), I threw up in the trash can in front of me. So what happened? It turns out, this had happened before and I remember it, too. It's called the vasovagal response, and it's when blood rushes out of the head for a brief amount of time, causing a small black-out. This usually happens when the person thinks about something disturbing to them too hard and too long. For me, it's been medical stuff. Now, I can think about medical things, but I can NOT think about blood, veins, pulses, or people's wrists. (You know the part on your wrist where you can see your veins? I cannot STAND it! I have to look away, and I can't even bring myself to make the gesture!)

The first time this happened was in sixth grade. I was reading an almanac about how to take your pulse from your wrist, and I was examining it for a long time, when I felt a strange sensation wash over me. I had never felt it before, so I knew it was time to turn the page. I had only just turned the page when I looked up and saw that my vision was all speckled. Have you ever walked out of a dark room into a bright room and your vision needs to adjust? That's what it looked like. I thought that was what was happening, but it wasn't. Next thing I know, I'm on the floor waking up. As I was getting up off the floor, it was hard to distinguish reality from fantasy. I couldn't tell if it was really happening. The first thing I heard someone say was, "His head looked all twitchy." When I got up, I asked, "What happened?" The teacher told me that I just fainted. It only lasted about two seconds. I was just reading a book, when BLAM! I just fall down immediately. The teacher also stated that I went pale, my eyes were still open, and my head twitched a little. I was taken to the nurse's after that. We went to the neurologist and he told us it was called the vasovagal response. So, fast-forward back to the present. After Christmas Break ended, I was EXTREMELY anxious to go back to school. Every day I was afraid that I was going to faint again. This lasted quite a long time, all the way until I went to see the psychiatrist. She prescribed me a medication that helped to relieve anxiety. It made me a bit drowsy at first, but it started to work a couple of weeks later. Soon enough, almost every day was fine. I still take it now, and I think it helps.

Actually, I know it helps, because it also worked for depression. I was convinced that there was nothing good about myself. When Dr. Gay would ask me if I thought there was anything good about myself, I would reply, "No, I can't think of anything." But today, I can think of a few different things, which is very rare on my part. It shows that I've come a long way from depressed to happy. That's still one thing, though: happy.

I claimed that I didn't know what being happy honestly felt like, and I still don't know if I ever have. Regardless, I've really progressed in getting past most of my depression. I might go into mental spirals on some days, but I don't go into them as much anymore. In conclusion, I've come very far in getting past my struggles.

10 Tomorrow

Well, I think this is it. I don't have much more to talk about, honestly. I feel like I've put all of my feelings into this book. But I think it doesn't need too much more. I know it may feel like the end shouldn't be here yet, and I think you're right. It may be the end of this book, but it's not the end of me. This is NOT the end. I believe we'll meet again sometime.

I hope I've helped shed some light onto my life, and some of Asperger's, too. Having Asperger's is what makes me, and I wouldn't trade having it for anything else. There are many successful people with Asperger's, and I plan to be one of them. But most of all, I hope I helped parents with autistic children. I hope that some of the info in this book will help you raise your child well, and I hope they become successful in life. And to any child with Asperger's or autism out there, you're not alone. I guarantee that at least one of you reading this book will think to yourself, "Hey, me too! That's exactly how I feel!"

Just know that you're not alone with your feelings, and that's something I even need to practice telling myself.

Anyway, that about wraps up this book. I'll most likely be writing more books, but for now, I'm going to take a break. This book has been about a year in the making, and a lot has changed along the way. I hope I've helped a lot of people, and if even one person's life has changed from this book, then I've done my job right.

Lastly, this isn't the last you'll be hearing from me. I'm gonna be around. And it's not the end of my life, either. At the time of me writing this, it's just several more days until eighth grade begins. for me. Maybe a lot will happen in that year. I don't know yet. A lot more things are going to happen to me, but I don't know what might happen. Who knows? Maybe something wonderful, maybe something terrible or maybe even something in between. Regardless, I'm going to push myself past any obstacle in front of me. But for now, I don't know, and no one else knows, what tomorrow may hold.

Nicolas Saliani is an author, video game enthusiast and avid chess player. Diagnosed with Asperger's at the age of five, he has learned to see the advantages of living on the autism spectrum. Passionate about helping others, he shares his personal experiences with behavior challenges, depression and obsessions giving insight into the mind of a teen with Asperger's.

Website: www.nsaliani.com
Email: nicolas.saliani@gmail.com

www.ingramcontent.com/pod-product-compliance
Lightning Source LLC
Chambersburg PA
CBHW061335040426
42444CB00011B/2929